Gardenia's Heart

A journey of the wandering soul

Zohreh Ansari

Serial Number: P2446100196
Title: Gardenia's Heart
Authors: Dr. Zohreh Ansari
Illustrators & Drawings: Dr. Zohreh Ansari
Layout: Monika Davis
ISBN:978-1-77892-105-6
Metadata: Poetry, Short Story
Book Size: Paperback, Royal
Pages: 158
Publication Date: May 2025
Publisher: Kidsocado Publishing House

Copyright © 2025 By Kidsocado Publishing House
All Rights Reserved, including the right of reproduction in whole or in part in any form.

Kidsocado Publishing House
Vancouver, Canada

Phone: +1 (236) 333-7248
WhatsApp: +1 (236) 333-7248
Email: info@kidsocado.com
Website: https://kidsocado.com
Address: 2100-1055 West Georgia St,
Vancouver, BC V6E 3P3, Canada

Beyond existence,
Beyond revelation
Beyond my loneliness and pain
Your Embrace!

In every melody,
With every song
A fresh start!

I find myself in you
My being, my solitude,

My Ultimate Joy! …

Dedicated:

**To Love
My Infinite Empire!**

Contents:

Preface *9*
My Sanctuary of Words *10*

Part One: Poetry

My Alchemy of Being (Kimia) *15*
Mehron *16*
Peace *17*
Only A Glimpse *18*
Longing Heart *19*
Untold Stories *20*
Eternal Serenade *23*
If One Day *26*
Time *28*
The Light We Miss *30*
Divine Beauty *32*
The Dove *33*
The Phoenix *35*
Belief *36*
A Journey Beyond *38*
Happiness *41*
Remnants of What Remains *43*
Sacred Secret *44*
Unchained Love *45*
The Blue Horizon *48*
Imagine If *49*
Splendor of Creation *52*
Finding Grace *54*
Eternal Flame *56*

In The Eyes of The Prey...................................... *58*
In Me, You Endure *60*
Dance of Fate *61*
Dust and Pain *63*
Forevermore *64*
In Your Eyes *65*

Part Two: Short Stories

The Awakening *68*
Hero *72*
Strive to Be Good *79*
Divine Light *85*
Happiness *90*
Time *96*
From Thorns to Petals *68*
Magic Pen *102*
Through Another's Eyes *107*
YOLO *109*
Opus of Life... *115*
The Golden Heart... *118*
A Stem in Love *122*
Everlasting Melody *126*
Stella *131*
Love's Secret Prayer *141*
Soulmate *143*
Last Chance *147*
Endless Love *150*
Gardenia's Heart *153*

Preface

Life is full of memories, fleeting moments slipping through our fingers. We assume they'll stay, waiting for their passing without truly holding them, carelessly letting them drift away.

For years, I've cast memories into the sea, releasing them like fish to swim far and free. Standing on the shore, I watched them sink deeper and deeper, gazing at the calm surface and the relaxed waves.

Until one day, someone asked me to dive deep into the water, finding my way to the ocean's heart. The waves disrupted the ocean's calm, and the fish, now frantic, swam back toward the surface.

Perhaps they will perish. Perhaps a storm will claim my serenity forever.

> Or maybe, just maybe, there's a reason.

> A message; My mission!

Gardenia's bright, white petals remind me of innocence and purity. They bring me hope and peace; they fill my heart with a sacred dream, a pure love.

This book has two chapters. First chapter on poems and second chapter on Short pieces and stories. In both chapters there are my Haiku, inspired by my son who has faith in my work.

My Sanctuary of Words

My first memory takes me back to fifth grade in elementary school, when among all my shining grades, I received an almost failing grade on my essay test. The school vice principal, along with my father, allowed me to retake the test. My brother guided me on how to write from my heart. On that day, I understood the meaning of belief and confidence, and I genuinely wrote about my feelings. That essay passed with honors!

The hope that emerged in my heart that day became a spark, igniting my sanctuary in writing. It was as if there was an essence within me—a river spirit—that had dried up.
Love poured like rain, and it flowed again. From that day, I knew: whenever I couldn't speak, I could write.

For years, words have been my safest haven. Each time, I discover a new world. Many times, I don't know how or why I write. Where did I start and when? But I write. Sometimes, a single sentence captivates me for hours. It's like I'm flying without wings. Interestingly, I'm afraid of heights, yet I love flying. Sometimes, I get lost in another world—a world different from this one, yet one I cannot fully comprehend.

In the journey of my life, I've met my heroes, the saviors of my soul. Each of them showed me the path to growth, and I will always be grateful to the Divine for what has been placed in my path.

I have been broken-hearted, thinking I would never heal.

Yet in every setback, a new window has opened to my heart. I name it LOVE. Yes! I think I am discovering my true self, and I am in love with it!

Along my path, I have written—from my heart and soul. Perhaps it's time to share. Perhaps some friends will read my words. Perhaps someone else will find their own world in mine and shed a tear or smile.

*** Zohreh. Spring 2025***

Amidst tears and poetry,
Your name, in love, I recite.
In me, you endure

Poetry

Kimia
My Alchemy of Being

In your warm embrace, a sacred place,
A haven that holds both soul and universe's grace

Expansive and nurturing, like an endless sea,
Enfolding all that is, and all that could be

In the depths of your gaze, a journey untold,
A mystical realm where new stories unfold

Born anew, in the land of love's sweet lore,
A tapestry woven on existence's floor

A realm they say, where streams with honey flow,
A timeless place, where the heart's secrets glow

Contemplating the alchemy in your eyes,
A dance with the unknown, under moonlit skies

In this chemistry, where time and being entwine,
A mystic potion, a love so divine

Mehron
My Joy, My Peace

Your smile, a soft light,
In the rain, my heart takes flight,
Wrapped in memories

Peace

I dream a dream, a dazzling truth
My soul in peace and serenity

We cruise through the storm, our memories
Children cherish for eternity

Over the land of daffodils
On the wings of a dove

I start a new voyage
Cradle the sky, up and above

I hold your hand, embrace your heart
What takes to cheer you up

Shall we sing proudly
The song that'll never stop

Only A Glimpse

Morning breeze, shimmering light on a dew
Walking the path, I never knew

The river running through my veins
My sorrows and hopes, my losses and gains

The river whispers tales untold,
Of dreams we chase, of hearts so bold

Yet in my chest, the echoes stay,
A child's heart, that never fades away

And tomorrow calls me, grown up; still in blank
Still the same kid, smiling, running by the river bank

Longing Heart

No deceits, no condemns, no battle do I wage,
Not of wood, nor thorn, and if not dust, then stone's my stage
I do not tremble in the shadows from the winter's cold,
No weeping, no cries from a heart so tightly hold

Neither storm, nor wave, nor flames of anger define,
No pain in my fantasies, no hatred's bitter brine,

No suffering from others, within my heart confined,
Only tears of longing and love in my eyes, entwined

Awake from dusk till dawn, like the moon's gaze,
Nightly illusions dance, sleepless in a restless haze

Sorrow, at times, befalls my soul, fragile and sore,
Yet sweetly, like a child, I find peace once more

In the hue of flowers, of spring's essence, rain's perfume,
Longing only for your love, in its sacred, sacred room

Every moment, every breath, with you far away,
My broken heart drifts with the wind, my soul ready to sway

Untold Stories

In my heart, a call I did make,
You arrived like a dream, no mistake

Fortunate rain in the desert's heart,
A sudden joy, a brand-new start

In the sorrow's dark, I stayed hushed,
Your eyes in mine, like the moon, blushed

In veiled secrets, my heart keeps aching,
Whispers between us, new desires waking

A fire in my sheaf, from wisdom's glow,
The world beneath, for you to know

I let you go, wishing forever to stay,
To share our tales, day by day

With every breath, a soulmate's grace,
Memories of our days, we embrace

Waiting in the curve of the horizon's might,
For night to escape, bringing your light

Night falling, with a smile, I say,
A hundred untold stories to convey

Our love is pure, my dear, so true,
You've come to paint my world anew

With every glance, my spirit sings,
In your embrace, my heart takes wings

At dawn, your scent flow,
A hope's drop from your eyes,
Intoxication

Eternal Serenade

In the tapestry of twilight, where the moon's gentle glow,
Sways with the rhythm of hearts that warmly know,

Why do we weep for the stars that silently depart?
When, in the canvas of our love, they forever chart

Why shed tears for the parting night's embrace?
When, in our hearts, it finds a sacred space

Why do we mourn the fleeting moments' flight,
When in love's embrace, they turn to light?

Why grieve for the winds that softly fade,
When, in our souls, their whispers are laid?

Let's not mourn in the garden where passion blooms,
Instead, let the petals whisper the secrets of our rooms

A lantern of love, casting soft, glowing light,
On the pages of our friendship, penned in the quiet night

As the symphony of our souls tenderly entwines,
Eternal, as the love that in our core defines

Through the tapestry of time, our love prevails,
A serenade that echoes in celestial trails

Dancing like butterflies, soft and pure,
A love so poetic, forever to endure

Dancing through shadows,
Whispers bind our lives as one—
Delight glows the way

If One Day

The breeze on the ocean
The waves kissing the shore
What is on the path
Who can see, or know more?

And asking again:
How much do I love you?
How little you think,
How little you know, too

"If one day the wind is confined within the fence,
Light trapped in the cage, and clouds bound in chains,
If one day the sun dies while waves kiss the shore
At that time, perhaps,
"Perhaps"!
I might not love you anymore...

Autumn's pallets spark,
In colors, losing your sight
Hearts see you clearly

Time

Time, the gentle lover, dances through the night,
Guiding each heartbeat with its soft, steady light

Upon life's swift steed, it moves with tender grace,
Teaching us to cherish each moment we embrace

With one hand, pluck the roses of love's sweet bloom,
With the other, nurture dreams that chase away gloom

In the golden palace where our hearts align,
Time whispers, "In your heart, let true love shine"

Tears, like rain, fall on hearts so true,
Only in love's embrace do they reveal their hue

In the fire of passion, during quarrels and strife,
How do we find the beauty of love in our life?

Yet, in this garden where souls intertwine,
We walk with care, hearts forever entwined

Hope is the flame that warms our coldest days,
The beacon of love in the darkest of ways

Through passing moments, in love's tender kiss,
We ponder the taste of both sorrow and bliss

In the cup of our romance, such sweetness we taste,
In this dance of souls, where no step goes to waste

The moon, from its trials, rises anew,
Transforming from crescent to full, just like me and you

Future hearts will look back, and they will see,
That our love, like the moon, was meant to be

The Light We Miss

In the emerald fields where I tread and ponder,
The flowers' beauty calls, yet we seldom wander

The sky stretches vast, a boundless, deep blue sea,
Yet we rarely lose ourselves in its majesty

The sun, so proud, its brilliance we forget,
Its golden light a beacon we seldom beget

The earth, a marvel, when we pause to see,
And the nightingale's song, moon's grace, stars' decree.

How fortunate am I to embrace what's true,
For without truth, no breeze would blow through

Loneliness would never shift to tender embrace,
For these are life's decrees, and hold a sacred place

Blue sky softly weeps,
Sunset paints a heart's soft cry—
Eyes smile, lips tremble

Your gaze, glorious,
Depth of breath becomes a sigh—
Just a short-lived flash

Divine Beauty

Autumn sits upon the horizon,
weeping romantically

And I, with longing eyes,
await the tulips beneath the snow

Beneath this blanket of snow,
I find a fresh spring!

Winter, the white knight,
the ambassador of pure love...

The Dove

I wish I were a dove, to the skies I'd soar,
To answer freedom's call and seek truth's lore.
In the vast blue heavens, a chance to be,
A dove not for beauty, but for purity

For silence, to pass through memory's gate,
Bitter and sweet, a tale of love and fate.
To join warm embraces, genuine and great,
I wish I were a dove, my own heart's mandate

To feel the thrill of taking flight,
To savor the joy of escaping the hunter's might.
To fear the talons of eagles, a daunting sight,
And in the arms of love, find soft respite

Yearning for the summit, with love so sweet,
In every wingbeat, in every leap,
A dove's experience, both shallow and deep,
In the kingdom of the skies, where stories seep

Zohreh Ansari

Mountain tears cascade,
Blazing hills, charred trees withstand—
Autumn's love unfolds

The Phoenix

What is this world but the shadow of a Phoenix,
A bird soaring high, beyond our reach,
While we chase only its momentary echoes,
Hunting shadows in the sky

And the Phoenix weeps,
For those who dare to open their hearts
Like waves returning to the ocean,
They find the joy of surrender

How blissful it is to embrace,
Love in its wholeness,
A unity vast and eternal

Belief

The rain is falling—
The kind sky knows mercy,
The gentle soil knows mercy

I seek a fresh belief,
A belief set free,
An endless belief

I will return,
Delve deeper,
Rise higher

With the scent of the breeze,
The leaves will dance,
And the rain
Will fall again

*Whispers, no loud screams,
Serenity, hearts glowing
Glamour in silence*

A Journey Beyond

In the hush of a breath, a silent sea,
Waves full of might, a majestic decree

Against the flow, a daring dive,
Into the silence where heartbeats thrive

"How long must one linger?" A soul implores,
Night's deathly grip, day's despairs it stores

A chest, aching beneath the weight of the night,
A plea to break free, to seek the light

A cold hand, a tired gaze
How long we shall stay in this maze?

Sorrows, like mountains, stare at the sky,
In ruins of love, art, and emotions lie

All pain stems from forgotten silence,
The foundation of grief, a haunting reliance

A need, a desire, but not to remain,
Only in parting, can one break the chain

"O soul in love, surrender thy essence,
Body and spirit, entrust them hence

*Rise once more! No time remains,
It's late, too late, break free from these chains"*

*Let's go, let's venture, let's not stay,
In the quiet hearts, there is a storm at bay*

*A step away from the crest of the sea,
In the arms of the sky, an eternity*

*A hill, not a mountain, toward the shore,
A step to take, a step, no more*

*Let's embark on this rhythmic quest,
A farewell to silence, a journey best*

*Hands entwined, let the rebellion start,
Leave the ruins, feel the beating heart*

*Let's cruise together, let's unite
A shared odyssey toward eternal light*

*As we voyage afar, let's understand
Leaving is not just parting from the land*

*It's a rhyming dance, a poetic spree
A journey beyond to set hearts free*

The seagull and the fish
Skies and depths, worlds apart
Faith; binding them close

Happiness

What is happiness, O most beautiful,
In the virtues of the soul, it's bountiful

What's more beautiful than you in this realm?
Selfless, born from your love, overwhelms

If your love is held within the heart,
Joy becomes yours, a work of art

Oh, the joy of friendship in abundance,
No duality, all one, a dance of transcendence

In the garden, delighted with cypress and breeze,
In leisure, finding a friend amidst the trees

In self-realization, seeing unity's glow,
All love and moonlight, in oneness, they flow

Life, born of love, vibrant and sweet,
On its table, reason's light, a feast to greet

Sensation, if within the heart and soul it dwells,
From seeking to astonishment, a journey that swells

With you, I speak of the marvels of the path,
Wondering where it comes from, who's its aftermath

Zohreh Ansari

*In the realm of awe, we fall as devotees,
Lost in wonder, freed from certainties"*

Remnants of What Remains

Buildings crumble,
Humans fade,
Earth and time reshape,
And our thoughts
Become whispers of memory

A remembrance
Of words spoken, deeds done—
And a regret
For what was left unsaid, undone

Sacred Secret

You whispered, "I love you with all my heart,"
The heart replied, to the sea, it did impart,

A secret shared with the gentle breeze,
A love that moved with effortless ease

The wind, in dance, carried it to the waves,
Our souls, entranced, were both slaves and braves

The secrets of love must gently be kept,
In whispers shared, where silence is swept

Thus, Romeo, in his endless plight,
And Juliet, bathed in the soft moonlight

The nightingale's song, a mournful plea,
The sea alone holds this secret, to be

Unchained Love

"They say life offers a challenge, a quest
Requiring courage to ask, and to invest

Was I braver or were you, destiny's decree?
A dance of courage, whose lead was it to be?

I pondered, did I choose, or did I let it flow?
An effortless surrender, to destiny's soft glow

I allowed the journey to weave its tale
Embracing the unforeseen, like a ship without a sail

In life's script, where plans failed to mold
A chorus of voices, clichés of the bold

"You can't," they chime, shedding duty's weight
The canvas of choice, a personal fate

In days gone by, I lived each breath with care,
A struggle, indeed, 'gainst life's grasp and despair

Yet, through wavering, a revelation unveiled
Love blossomed within, and life's burdens paled

Midst this symphony, a whisper arose
"Let go," it beckoned, and I shed my prose

Not seeking possession, desires unconfined
An aching, courageous and romantically entwined

An aspiration, not for possession but delight
A wish for happiness, in the sun's warm light

Not mine, but ours, with souls intertwined,
No words needed, where hearts and spirits bind

True love bestowed, a gift divine
A fusion of spirits, a celestial sign

The divine within me, crystallized and clear
To love and be loved, the essence sincere

Yet, within this feeling, a revelation unveiled
A weed within, in vanity, exhaled

A cage of love unwittingly created
An "I" emerged; love's purity abated

Oh, divine, lend me a guiding hand
To preserve his joy, let love withstand

Not to possess, but to see him thrive
In his heart, my love shall be alive

In silence, in solitude, revelations unfold
To seek his desire , his love to share and hold

A relinquishment, a tearful release
A poetic farewell, a soothing peace"

The Blue Horizon

To live in beauty, one may strive,
See the world through beauty's eyes

In the heart of the night's embrace,
Let the moonlight on hearts trace

With the breath of memories, one can soar
Into spring gardens, each night, once more

If only you could witness the sight,
Even stones crack in the cold night

In every house, if one could see,
No light but purity and loyalty

If only one could embark and sail,
With a timber boat, beyond the veil

To the horizon, where the sea meets sky,
A world of blue, where dreams do lie

Mirror of hearts, in blue array,
People and places, all in the sway

Clear and free from weariness,
In a world where everything is blue, no less

Imagine If ...

If in the realm where Adam trod,
Only kindness led the way to God

If Satan's words, divine and clear,
Unveiled to all, with no trace of fear

If the unkind hands ceased their cruel play,
Pharaoh's blades put peace on display

If darkness and anger held no sway,
The beauty of love untouched, in the light of day

If in an orphan's eyes, tears unfurled,
Tyrants' hearts pierced by an innocent world

If in a war-torn night, under the moon's gaze,
Weapons discarded, peace ablaze

If we did not fight over faith's divide,
All of us would be in God's region, side by side

If forgiveness echoed the first mistake,
Loyalty's pact, a life at stake

If harsh words vanished from the air,
No place for weapons, no swords to bear

If wounds of the tongue found no fame,
Swords infolded, no sorrow to claim

If temptation ceased with no voice to call,
No devil's whisper, no darkened thrall

If foul words found no space to reside,
Honesty's kiss, with love as its guide

If each smile shone with sincerity bright,
Words that bloom like flowers in light

If beautiful words painted sincerity's art,
Genuine smiles from each heart

If truth's aroma in words was found,
Swords' wounds, an empty sound

If kisses carried selfless grace,
Sincere smiles lit each face

If spoken words bore truth's scent,
Helping hands to others lent

If every heart burned with love's fire,
Eternal beauty each soul would admire

If we, unified in a human embrace,
Our lives would be bonded, with sweetest grace

We together, in love's embrace,
Could lift this world to a harmonious place

Splendor of Creation

What difference does it make?
If you are a green leave, still on a branch,
And I, a yellow one on the ground,
If I am red, dancing with the wind?
Cheering today, gone tomorrow!

What difference does it make?
To which color we turn,
And to which color we fade?

You and I, born from the same tree,
Rooted in the same soil!
Swept away by the same wind,
In the heart of one soil, we'll turn to dust

I love you, with all the colors of life,
You are with me,
The beautiful manifestation of existence,

The splendor of creation,
The magnificence
In our beautiful colors,
Beside each other

And a day will come
When on the emptiest road
Only a recollection of children's footprints remains

A day will come
When from waterfalls
Only traces on the faces of stones are seen

In an evening not so far away
The pond, drained of the moon's gaze
Figs wither on the branches

You and I
And the little garden;
Only a memory..."

Finding Grace

My world, a garden; evergreen,
Time flowing like a gentle stream

I take my breaths with a sigh so deep,
In this ephemeral place we keep

Nothing but the ache of separation's bond,
Grief profound, in hearts so fond

The pain of this world, so keen,
Apart from the love that lies between

Friends' hearts, with seeds of pain,
In this realm, their sorrows reign

Yet in the desert, there's a place,
Where swaying reeds find their grace

In joy's garden, nightingales sing,
Amidst the stars, laughter rings

Moonlight dances, Venus gleams,
In my celestial, joyful dreams

Whispers in the breeze
Poppies bloom in love's warm arms
Hummingbirds sing free

Eternal Flame

You ignited a fire within my heart,
With a tender gaze, a loving start

Unaware that the bird of your love,
Rests in the embrace of my heart, like a dove

You wanted to immerse me deep,
In the fountain of your tear's sweep

Unaware you drowned in silent streams,
The tears I cried in broken dreams

You tried to break me with love's sweet call,
Whispering lies beneath it all

I clearly see the lies you weave,
Yet still, my heart chooses to believe

I forgive you, my dear, with peace and grace,
By love's pure flame, I find my place

Though blame once lingered in your name,
My heart's still burning an eternal flame

In the Eyes of The Prey

*He nocked the arrow to the bow,
With steady aim, breathing so slow*

*The gazelle turned, her gaze serene,
In the hunter's eyes, a curious scene*

*Aren't you afraid of death, dear prey?
Why not flee? Why choose to stay?*

*The hunter pondered this cruel game,
A dance of fate, both wild and tame*

How unfair, this tragic plight!
She knows not of fear, nor the threat of night.

In her innocence, she stands so still,
Unaware of the hunter's icy will

He lowered the bow, the arrow's threat,
Entranced by her beauty, his heart was set

As he gazed into her eyes so clear,
He found a reflection of his own hidden fear

How calm the waters of the pond might be?
Mirroring truths of what's yet to see

In that moment, the world dashed away,
Two souls entwined in the light of the day

In Me, You Endure

Autumn, another chilly season,
In the midst of colors,
My eyes lose you amongst the colors,
Yet, in my heart, I see you

I seek you from every direction,
Wherever the wind carries,
In the dance of branches and leaves,
With a tender kiss, I pluck you

Silent and alone every dawn,
Your memory in my embrace,
Like the sweet essence of life,
In every breath, I feel you

Dance of Fate

May my verses capture this grace,
Where beauty dances in a spring's embrace

The world, a garden rich and bright,
In bloom of life's unending light

Yet, in this splendor lies a sigh,
A bittersweet, relentless cry

For parting's pain and longing's ache
Are shadows that our hearts shall take

In parting's ache and joy's warm grasp,
Our souls' profoundest depths unmask

The garden's peace, where nightingales sing,
And stars above with soft light bring

In celestial fields where solace lies,
Through the heart of the endless skies,

We find our souls' serene delight,
In joy's embrace, through darkest night

My words seek to hold the span,

Zohreh Ansari

Of human trials, of life's grand plan

Through highs and lows, the dance of fate,
In beauty's grace, we contemplate

Dust and Pain

I needed you to walk by my side, my dear,
Barefooted, without a hint of fear
Dust of the road upon our faces laid,
As my steadfast companion, unafraid

It's only a dust that softly flies,
Veiling heavily our sunlit eyes.
Though wounds from the stony path may ache,
They're gentler than the soaring dust's wake

You, my companion, a solace true,
As we tread the path, just we two
Dust may dance, wounds may bear,
Yet, together, we bravely dare

In the journey where footsteps roam
With you, my dearest, I find home
For in the midst of dust and pain,
Our shared love becomes our gain

Forevermore

In the morning breeze, a lover's sigh,
Through the curls of the meadow, a gentle tie

To capture the heart's kindness, unfurl,
From the dust of the earth, let a hundred songs swirl

A song sung by all, a harmonious embrace,
A hundred signs of love, adorned with grace

Waiting for the dawn to break its sleep,
Hope sparks in the heart's dwelling, deep

Wandering in the garden, a ballad unfolds,
The nightingale sings, a tale of love it holds

As the scent of blossoms heralds the spring,
A garden blooming with a thousand stories to bring

Seated amidst the petals' soft embrace,
For a mother's love, a tribute to grace

One day, perhaps, my name fades away,
That day, in memories, let my name sway

In Your Eyes

In your eyes, I wake to dawn,
Through a glass I look,
Where our beautiful love is drawn

Whispers of rain, secrets untold,
In your gaze, my heart takes hold

Moments lingering; filled with grace,
Yearning in each silent space

Restless, longing for your touch
I leave you, still
Loving you so much

Short Stories

The Awakening

In the beginning, God created Man...

At the birth of the first dawn, a blossom opened its lips in laughter. A breeze whispered through the heart of nature.

"This is my masterpiece."

Hearts were pure, untouched by pretense. Virtue was the only purpose—truth so sacred it needed no words. In those days, God was content, and a man's word was his honor. There were no shadows. Only a golden sea of sunlight, where raindrops danced together, and deer ran freely—no fear, no pursuit.

Everything was beautiful. Everyone was at peace.
In those days, only two words rose above all:

Friendship; Love.

But then, a breeze shifted. And with it came a shadow. A restless thought drifted skyward, weaving dreams from fleeting imagination. And that thought took shape. That shadow became many things.

"I" was born.

The "I" within me, untamed and unaware, lost itself in its own depths. It hid behind words.
Drunk on the wilderness of unconscious longing, I was lured by desire, adorned in the ornaments of tradition—yet blind to truth.

Soon, that "I" claimed my life. It seized my conscience. Behind a mask of anger, it wore pride, prejudice, fear.

Compassion became a stranger. For a long time, my eyes remained closed. But eventually I awoke. Aching to change, I felt a warmth stir within me. A forgotten kindness blossomed in my soul. And I began to transform.

I wanted to mend what the "I" had broken. I knelt beside a wilting flower, eager to offer water. But the flower whispered:

> "With which hands? Are these not the same hands that left me to thirst?"

I reached for a fallen leaf. The tree murmured:

> "How? You nourish barren fields with neglect."

I tried to hold the hand of an orphan. He sighed:

> "Are these the same hands that once brought pain? Do you offer love now—or pity?"

The "I" within me had no answer. And I saw clearly how I had wounded so many hearts. But then, like the first light of dawn, my conscience stirred. It rose from years of silence, and slowly, the dust of darkness began to fall away, revealing the hidden beauty beneath.

I longed to wrap myself in love, for all that is beautiful, for all that is noble. I wanted to burn so brightly that I would dissolve into the very essence of love itself.

My soul ached. Yet even in the suffering, I found mercy.

Even in the sorrow, there was light. My heart dreamed of waiting eyes, of a heartbeat reaching toward me through distance.

Toward that yearning, I took a step, to meet the quiet joy of another soul.

In my despair, I wondered:

Should I laugh or cry at the death of compassion?

I weep for a world lulled to sleep.

For hearts grown cold. Even as laughter echoes, will there be any tears left for the loss of tenderness?

Any smile left for kindness now gone? Still, I seek it, in the beauty of a laugh, in the rhythm of a melody, in the warmth of a kiss, or the gentle curve of a loose strand of hair.

Days drift by. My heart, heavy with longing, sips from the cup of a soul that still burns. I meet an ascetic, humble-faced, who offers me a crust of bread.

And it becomes a feast. His smile holds a harmony—of joy, of sorrow, of love, of passion—in a single breath.

Yes, I have tasted the sweetness of laughter, the beauty of weeping from love. Of loving, and being loved.

I have lived it, all in the depth of a single, timeless moment. And now, **I feel God.**

In every breath.

In every cell.

In all of my being.

Fearing the mirror
Standing lonely, blue heron
Secret shadows loom

Hero

In the hustle and bustle of days and nights, within the turbulence of thoughts, I ask myself: "Have I ever taken any wrong path? What is the definition of good and bad? Is goodness or badness real or a virtual conception? A lot of times we lay out a plan for every day of our lives, and sometimes we just let it take its course. What is the goal? Where is the end?"

Wandering in limbo, I try to find an answer. And then I decide that everyone's existence has a reason. The idea that perhaps I shouldn't have gone somewhere, shouldn't have told someone, I wish...

Again, I ask myself: "what is existence? Our existence, this universe? Why each of us are in the position that we are? Along my path, I've passed by people indifferently, and sometimes I've stopped without knowing why, and greeted a stranger. It has happened many times that while immersed in my own thoughts, someone I didn't know smiled at me and invited me into their world of joy; a familiar smile from a so called unfamiliar, unknown savior (and can I really say they are unknown or stranger? Aren't we all parts of the same big flame?)"

We spend our entire lives waiting for a miracle to happen; waiting for an extraordinary happening. We fix our eyes on the sky, hoping that an angel will descend with its white wings and deliver a special message to us: "O most chosen one! Heaven is yours!"

And we forget that the miracle of life greets us every morning and every night in the embrace of the rising sun, and the calming glow of the moonlight. We forget that every breeze, every raindrop, every leaf that grows on a branch, every season, and every color; every moment, and every breath we take is a miracle! Our very existence is a unique event, and we don't even notice it. We forget that the kindest angels don't have wings, and with a smile, a prayer, or a wish, they silently fly into our hearts.

We search for a legendary hero, Unaware that heroes and angels walk among us every day, Shaping our lives in quiet, extraordinary ways.

The angel who, with the first smile of morning, sends a photo of the neighbor's tree, captioned softly, "The neighbor's tree greets autumn, And I am thinking of you."

The angel who cups two delicate hands in prayer, offering it to us with tear-filled eyes, and whispers, "My dear friend, every morning, I hold God in my hands and pray for you."

The angel who doesn't wait for words of need, but checks on you, day after day, their care unspoken, but deeply felt.

The angel who, upon hearing you're unwell, quietly prepares the comforting meal of your childhood, And brings it to your door, Finding any excuse just to see you smile.

The angel who stays by your side at any cost, without obligation. And one day, silently and calmly, they leave. They leave simply because they love you... they let you go and leave.

And sooner or later, you realize that the simple people in your life were the real heroes. Heroes whose names are not written in history books, but who make history every day. Heroes whose presence becomes ordinary, repetitive, and maybe even exhausting.

And sooner or later, you realize that every day, someone was taking you to a banquet with God. You realize that paradise exists! Paradise had been right here all along. It was never lost! God never cast us out of it. We simply lost our vision.

Every night, we stand together, whispering as dawn approaches. A gaze that witnesses miracles unfolding every moment, though it doesn't realize it. I remember when I was a child, sitting in the yard on warm summer nights, staying up late, sometimes lying on the wooden benches, gazing at the stars. We would try to find the Big Dipper and the Pleiades. We pointed to the North Star. Sometimes, I would say I found Venus, and my brother, with his playful charm, would tease me, saying, "Venus is a planet!"

But soon, to win my heart, he would say, "In this vast sky, you have a shining star; we have nothing, no name, no fame!" And we would all laugh.

Back then, like everyone else, I had imaginary heroes and wanted to be one of them someday. One day, I wanted to be the world's best gymnast, like Nadia Comăneci. Another day, I dreamt of being Loui Pasteur. Sometimes, I thought it would be so simple to be Avicenna, and I would write not just two books, but many more. My father loved poetry, he used to read Rumi, Khayam and Hafiz, and he often spoke of Women Poets. For a while, I decided I would be one. When my brother decided to become a physician, I thought it was the best job in the world! After seeing the art of calligraphy, another passion ignited within me. The first time I saw Richard Clyderman playing the piano, my soul soared. I wanted to be all of them, but I didn't know which one to choose. I wanted to be someone great!

Years passed, slipping by before I understand that no act of goodness is too small or insignificant. It took years to realize that to achieve something great, one doesn't need to be a great person; it's the size of your heart that matters. Years went by before I came to understand that the people in books, or behind the masks of fame, are not always what they seem.

Years passed, before I finally understand that each smile I encountered was hiding a secret—an unspoken truth.

And then one day, it dawned on me! "I just want to be an ordinary person; Simple! I just want to be me!" In that moment, I realized how difficult that decision truly was.

The true stories in History are shaped by people like you and me. People who their actions and words, their very presence and sometimes their departure, changed the course of others' lives, especially the lives of those close to them. They offered inspiration through love and kindness, shared thoughts of goodness, or painted images of what shouldn't be done or how not to live.

It took years to grasp that it was the simple, ordinary people in my life who shaped me into who I am.

'My true heroes.' The ones who simply were themselves. Those who quietly shared every breath with me, sometimes battling their own demons, sometimes embodying the spirits of kings and warriors. They too, like Achilles and Alexander, have taken up their bows and fought the great battles of life. like Romeo and Juliet have woven love stories of their own; without ever needing to have their tale immortalized in books or legends.

Sometimes we act out of love without thinking, and one day the consequence of that action becomes another entity. The truth is: everyone is the hero of a story already written, a hero who doesn't even know...

I used to ask how is that possible? My father said: "Just put a bit of your soul into what you do!"

I know people who invest a bit of their soul in helping others every day, every moment. A bit of their soul in a smile, a movement, a query, a sincere and pure presence, and they do it so quietly. They are my true Heroes...

My Heroes; Are the ordinary loving people with pure hearts, whose names may not be in the books, but without them no book was ever scripted ...

My Heroes; Are People whose existence paints this world as a beautiful painting. The beautiful hall of existence...

People whose existence makes seeing and breathing worthwhile...

My Heroes; Have fell and risen. Have burnt and yet smiled. They have felt pain and embraced love...

Zohreh Ansari

Morning dew, flowers
Embracing as sparrows chirp
Spring dreams in silhouette

Always Strive to Be Good

I was twelve years old when I asked my brother to leave a note in my journal. Truthfully, I felt a little shy, worried he might think it was one of those silly, girlish things. So, I quickly changed my request and asked him to write me a piece of advice instead. At that time, my brother was twenty-two years old. Despite his youth, his friends and family called him "The Wise Elder!" His room overflowed with the magic of world and Persian classical literature. I think he had some sort of arrangement with the publishing companies because he always seemed to know about new releases before the ink had even dried.

I can still picture his bookshelf: the top shelf on the right, with Jean-Christophe by Romain Rolland in four volumes, Jean-Christophe again, this time in seven volumes, War and Peace, Les Misérables... Charmed, The Ten-Thousand-Year History of Iran, collections by famous Persian author, Samad Behrangi, and countless others.

Every year for our birthdays, he would give my sister and me the latest books published by the Institute for the Intellectual Development of Children and Young Adults. He would hide the books under his bed weeks before our birthdays, teasing us with stories: "I forgot this year!" Or, "My university textbooks cost too much," or, "Car repairs drained my budget." Every moment with him felt vibrant and full of surprise.

I knew asking him to write in my journal was a long shot, but I tried again, "Please, just write something for me?"

He looked at me and my notebook, asking, "What's the point of all this? What good will it do you?"

I replied, "It'll be useful someday." But when he looked into my eyes, I blurted out the truth: "Well… all my friends have one!"

He smiled—a genuine, warm smile. The honesty of my answer must have touched him. He took my notebook and flipped through it. "It's empty! No one's written anything yet," he remarked.

"I want you to be the first," I said, eager.

He cleared his throat, "Alright, but don't get too sappy. You know I don't like that." Yet, I could tell he was pleased. He knew how much he meant to me.

After thinking for a moment, he said, "Fine. Just one sentence!"

"Okay, thank you!" I exclaimed, thrilled.

He handed me back the notebook. In his beautiful handwriting, he had written:

"Always Strive to Be a Good Person, Everywhere You Go"

It was short but powerful. I had his words, his handwriting, his signature—a new treasure. I didn't ask him what being "good" meant. In my childlike way, I thought I knew. It seemed simple: just don't be bad.

I proudly collected more entries in the days that followed. My sisters, friends, a few of my teachers, even the school principal wrote something. Within two weeks, my journal was filled with over forty pieces of advice, poems, joyful messages, and loving notes. But I always regretted not having the courage to ask my parents to write in it too.

My journal from when I was twelve became a precious companion. Every time I opened it, I read his words:

"Try to be a good person, always and everywhere!"

As the years went by, I realized that living up to those words was one of the hardest challenges in life.

Thirty years passed…

It was early morning on the first day of the new year. I was visiting my brother and his lovely wife, Maryam. The house was quiet; everyone else was still asleep. My brother and I decided to go out for bread and get breakfast started. The morning sun was warm, the breeze refreshing. It had been ages since we had gone out together early mornings.

We didn't talk about the past, instead drifting into the world of poetry and music. Though he played his guitar less often now, his taste in music was still impeccable, and he knew melodies more beautiful than any I had ever heard. I praised his knowledge, and he shook his head, "Ah, there isn't much time left for art anymore. I should devote more time to it."

I reminded him of the advice he had once written for me. He laughed. "Did it help you?" He asked, still remembering.

"It was so hard," I admitted. "I didn't manage it." Then I asked, "Can you give me some new advice? This time, it's not for show. I really need it."

His deep, calm blue eyes met mine, and he smiled.

"I'm still on this journey myself," he said. "But remember, every word, every action has a purpose… a single meaning." Then he added:

"Live in such a way that every morning, you won't be ashamed of the face you see in the mirror."

Every morning, I smile in the mirror. Once again he took me to a world beyond my imaginations. I ponder the meanings of good and bad. I still strive to understand what it truly means to be a good person. It's not easy, but I keep trying...

Floating clouds gliding
A lonely wave dancing free
Spring smiling in the breeze

Divine Light

In the face of difficulties, children's first saviour is their tears. The day came when this arena no longer applied to me! It wasn't about the joy of new year's clothing, white shoes, or a leather-bound notebook anymore. This time, I faced red lines that couldn't be erased with any eraser, and I thought to myself, "Have I done anything wrong or broken any heart or…. what did I do to deserve this?

When I realized I couldn't do anything to change fate, my initial reaction was denial. It was impossible that the world would mark me with such a destiny, why me? Out of all the people? When I understood that there was no escape, I became angry! Angry at myself and those dearest to me. I lashed out at those who may have suffered more than me in the fire of grief. But gradually, I grew tired. I withdrew calmly and wrapped a curtain of depression and sorrow around myself like a web.

Little by little, I understood that I am not a separate interwoven fabric; why not me? What made me different? Then I accepted it; and silently waited for days without any motive or even pain and sorrow. Like an empty floating log, light! I danced with the wave, sang with every breath, and simply went on and on…

And then, I met her! Her LIGHT opened my heart!

...Meeting Nora was one of the best events in my life. She loved everything and everyone, she loved life without being attached to it! She could find beauty in everything, not to get intoxicated by it but to recognize and acknowledge.

Those days, I sat in her mythology sessions, reviewing the faces of all the students. Everyone was looking for something, sometimes with a reason and sometimes without! She talked about love, about divine beauty, about how these two create the structure of existence in the world and take their place in the hierarchy. Nora spoke of prophets, leaders, of gods, and then each of us placed in the position of gods without knowing we were there. The truth was not hidden in the Quran or Rumi verses, nor in Jung's books, nor in theology. It hadn't been hidden anywhere else. The search had to be continued elsewhere! In the deepest layer of one's own soul, where they used to say it's as if someone is knocking, as if it's falling into a well, it's as if you're being possessed by love! And at that exact moment, the tranquility of the world falls into your heart because you know the most beautiful feeling belongs to you, the feeling of freedom...

In the midst of bitter and sweet moments of life, Noora was sent to save my soul. A dormant being inside me had gone to sleep, all my feelings were the same, the world had no variety, and everything had a normal color; until one day, Light spoke to me. If all paths were supposed to be open to me, and I wouldn't experience suffering, where would I find the beauty of the path? If every challenge in life were to take me off balance, where would I stand?

On a rainy and cold winter afternoon, Nora began a new chapter: "Lord Krishna is believed to embody tenderness, patience, compassion, and love. He symbolizes the divine protection of humanity. Krishna is not limited to a physical form; he exists everywhere—from the smallest micro-organism to the largest animal, from an atom to the entire universe. To perceive him, one must use the mind, for he is energy, a spirit that transcends form."

One of the students interrupted, "Is it true that you can find Krishna in a deer's eyes?"

My thoughts began to wander. Just a few days ago, I had encountered a deer in the woods. It was so close that I could gaze directly into its eyes. The mesmerizing beauty and innocence within them reminded me of my daughter's large, dark eyes.

With a sincere yet gentle tone, Nora replied, "Every Spirit Guide offers unique wisdom and inspiration. The spirit of the deer teaches us to be kind, gentle, compassionate, and loving—to ourselves and to others. Deer guide us to choose kindness, unconditional love, and peace. The deer's eyes are bright and clear, reflecting back at us like a mirror. To find Krishna, you must see with your mind and spirit, for he is never far from you."

She looked at me and smiled. "Seek your Krishna in Kimia!"

I held my breath, unable to stop the tears from welling up. Once again, Nora had opened the doors to my heart, flooding it with light. She has been the beacon of hope and happiness, the guide to serendipity not only for me, but for anyone who knows her.

Between crawling on the ground and standing on shaky, uncertain feet, I chose to stand. Her light took my hand, filled me with kindness, and guided me toward peace. I made peace with life, accepting the world and everyone in it just as they are.

The tears that fell that day were tears of liberation—my soul breaking free from the confines of a narrow body. I entered a world my spirit had always belonged to, though I had been lost in it. In that moment, I understood that God, or Krishna—whatever name one chooses—had always been right here, within my grasp. This divinity was mine, and no religion or ritual could ever take it away from me.

My tears were no longer the battlegrounds of childhood memories. Instead, each teardrop became a river of a sea I had not known was within me. I had connected with a world brimming with beauty. I embraced the child within me, knowing how fragile she was, yet realizing how strongly my love could protect her.

My feelings have a lot to say; I like to hear, see, learn, write, and share...

Once again Happiness has touched my soul ...

Happiness

Sitting by the stream, I let my thoughts take me to my far memories and dreams. The colorful autumn leaves dance around in the fall breeze. Angela is sitting beside me, smiling: "isn't it all so joyful?"

A few steps away, a group of children, no more than five or six years old, run and laugh in the rain, not worried about getting soaked. Unburdened by so many worries, carefree about the future. Though, who really knows? Maybe they do have dreams, just like me.

I drift into my memories. As a child, I wished I could run fast like my sister, but parting from my beloved hopscotch game was always too difficult for the chubby little girl of our house. When school began, my biggest concern was finishing the year with the top grades. I'm not sure if it was for my own pride or my parents'. Was the feeling of accomplishment for their joy, mine, or both?

As a teenager, I dreamt of becoming someone important someday. The meaning of "important" back then was so different! Time reveals many of life's tricks: one day, you realize that every actor on this grand stage is both significant and insignificant.

My youth was so busy that I can't quite recall what I truly wanted. Everything and nothing. One day filled with anxiety, another with joy, another spent waiting for tomorrow, sometimes even waiting for a miracle. Counting down hours and days to grow up was a childhood habit most of us indulged in, unaware that one day those past moments would become the lost wishes we'd yearn for…

I take a deep breath, letting it fill my lungs. The scent of autumn seeps into my soul, a gentle reminder of change and memory. My father once said, "When you wish to journey with your thoughts, close your eyes and let your heart lead the way."

I remember how as autumn set in, everyone's mood changed. Some were preoccupied with the realization that more than half the year had passed, and there was still so much left undone. Others busied themselves with preparations for the New Year. Some made plans for the cold season ahead…

But in those gentle autumn days, all those worries faded with the sound of the stream and the coolness of the breeze, if only for a brief moment, transforming into a fragrance called life! Everyone knew these colors and leaves held a different message, an invitation to embrace each moment, to walk over rustling leaves, to sit on wooden benches by the pond, and to seek warmth in the sunbeams that smiled through the clouds.

The scent of rain-soaked leaves, the soft murmur of the waterfall—it feels like just yesterday, right here!

Early mornings, wooden benches, freshly brewed tea, and a few boiled eggs. The aroma of hot porridge! Cinnamon!

Sometimes, memories are so vivid that the line between dreams and reality blurs. I've often asked myself: Which is real, and which is only a sweet dream? Where should we search for happiness? In the colorful fantasies of the past, in today's moments, or in the perhaps impossible, but sweet, dreams of tomorrow?

The sounds of life's bustle echo in the distance. Behind this little stream and forest park; noises of the vehicles. I open my eyes. Raindrops gently land on my cheeks.

Through the clouds, a streak of sunlight appears. The breeze weaves through the branches, showering me in golden rain. The caress of the water's song...

Soon, winter's cold breath will fill the air, and the earth will sleep under a blanket of snow. But it won't be long before the blossoms of life break through the cold ground. The springs will overflow once again, and the mulberry branches will bear fruit. And so, the cycle continues, with a lingering sense of expectation!

Angela breaks the silence:

Time has gifted us mindfulness— the true manifestation of happiness. I've both lost and found happiness as I've wandered through life's maze. I've discovered it in the heights of sorrowful moments, amidst tears and despair. I know I will lose it again, cry like a child once more, and fall asleep longing for it. In dreams, I will see the letters of happiness etched on a stone, on a wall, in the narrow alleys of the past, or in the pure, innocent eyes of a sapling.

And suddenly, I will wake. In my deepest joy, in my loneliest moment, I will realize that somewhere far away, in another time, someone with a heart—simply put, a love—belongs to me, is mine. And that is enough.

Happiness comes from within and reveals itself in a gaze. It's in hearing the laughter of a neighbor's child, in witnessing two hearts finding each other, in the embrace of the sunset, and in discovering moonlight reflecting off the dark pond of night. Happiness is when you can look at the world with gratitude, free from envy. It's when you can see yourself as small and be humbled by life.

Happiness is when, even amidst deep sorrow, a smile graces your lips. It's found in sharing your joy with an open heart. Happiness is when a loved one trusts you with a secret, and you hold that secret close, bearing it on your shoulders and shedding a tear. It's in the desire to strive, to keep seeking even when you haven't found what you're looking for. Happiness is the courage to say, "I'm sorry, I made a mistake," and the strength to forgive, to let go, and move forward.

Happiness is being consumed by love—unconditional, without "ifs" or "whys." It's being content with the world, afflicted with love's beauty. Being happy is both incredibly difficult and remarkably simple. To cherish each moment for its own sake, to know that this moment belongs to us—that is happiness.

The world does not gift us happiness; we seize it. Happiness is the art of finding joy in simple things. It is the art of seeking, finding, and then learning to let go.

I've found happiness in the scarcest times and places.

The world doesn't gift us happiness in a cup. We pour our essence into the empty vessel of this world. Then the world overflows with our zest, brimming with love.

Angela is quiet. I take a deep breath. My breath fills with happiness. There is no room for regret; everything I desire weaves into my being. Each breath carries my dreams, dreams born from love. The scent of orange blossoms fills the air. My countless blessings ...

Autumn, golden locks
Gardens adorned, pines ponder
Spring spirit lingering

Time

The sun was high above, radiant and proud, casting its warm, golden glow over the land. My soul wandered; 'what a lovely scenery, such a beautiful garden, yet not knowing what to do.' Time was my teacher, whispering wisdom: how to reach out and pluck a delicate flower without crushing its bloom, how to cradle tender buds so they could grow and flourish, how not to wound hearts or mar the beauty of existence, and how never to allow despair to take root in one's being.

I meandered along the garden's path, the earth humming beneath my feet, rich with secrets waiting to be discovered. Flowers burst forth in a vibrant riot of colors, but too often, they were passed without a moment's pause, I took their splendor for granted. Above, the sky stretched infinitely, a vast expanse holding dreams and mysteries, but how rarely did anyone seek to understand its endless blue or savor the wonder of its horizons!

I stopped and marveled at the symphony of life. The nightingale's song echoed in the air, each note a melody of hope, while the moon, shimmering like a queen draped in silver, cast an ethereal light upon the world. Stars sparkled in their cosmic dance, each twinkle a reminder of the universe's unfathomable grace. The sunlit day and the star-kissed night wove a delicate balance, a rhythm that so few took the time to notice.

A sense of gratitude swelled in my heart. The truth of life lay in the small things, the whispering breeze that caressed tired souls, the loneliness that transformed into unexpected, deep connections, the natural order that breathed kindness into existence.

I knew that it was these lessons, these whispers of time, that illuminated the path. They offered hope—the treasure of goodness and kindness, the force that anchored humanity and salvaged it from the brink of despair. The truths became beacons, leading the way through shadows, teaching my lost soul to see the beauty in the ordinary and to cherish the connections forged along life's path.

With a fervent heart, I took a silent prayer:

> *"O bird of my soul, before your final flight,*
>
> *Sing forth the joy of my awakened heart,*

As if in answer, the wind rustled through the trees, spreading colors onto the leaves with its cool, crisp breath, painting the garden with the hues of hope. Life's beauty continued to unfold, waiting for every soul to stop, breathe, and truly live.

From Thorns to Petals

Her day began with the same familiar ritual every morning. Joy would glance at the tall pine tree outside her window. Its green, strong presence was a silent reminder of her being alive. She'd smile and whisper, "Good morning, life. I still have another chance."

Beside her bed laid a note, a gentle nudge toward living mindfully: One good deed, one minute of reading, one new insight, one minute of exercise, one minute of music, and one deep breath. With determination, she took that breath, feeling the air fill her lungs and attempting to focus.

"Alright," she thought, "One breath at a time." She counted softly, "Inhale… 1, 2, 3, 4… hold… exhale 1, 2, 3, 4, 5, 6, 7." She repeated this, taming her restless thoughts.

"Today, I'll visit the library," she decided, feeling a surge of hope. 'Maybe I'll walk there. I have time.' But as she set off, she knew the challenge: fighting the chaotic thoughts that had been haunting her. Memories of past regrets and unanswered questions threatened to consume her. She needed to focus, to avoid the temptation of blaming others, the hardship of the gloomy memories that still stung.

The walk to the library took an hour, her mind flickering between memories and the present. She thought of the last time she had been there, not alone but walking beside someone who once meant everything to her. They had admired the birds, but his attention had always been elsewhere, distracted. Joy flew in her memories. That day the acacias had bloomed, and he had said, 'Don't take life so hard. Isn't this scenery too beautiful to be upset? Joy could never tell him how hard has been to give up so many things just to be able to be there with him for a moment. Her feelings were sacred, how could she share them if they were not mutual? Also, she didn't want to burden him with more dilemma or worries. He never asked her why she was sick and why she had to go to the hospital. He was too busy ...

The thought made her heart ache. She took another deep breath, fighting back the lump in her throat. I loved you. What did I miss? She wondered.

She repeated affirmations to calm herself: "Move on. You can. It's all in the past." Her feet carried her forward, step by step. She started Humming cheerfully.

At the library entrance, an elegant, old lady with a cane approached. The woman's face was lined with age, her lips pressed into a thin, bitter line. Her short, white hair was neatly styled, and despite the years etched on her skin, remnants of beauty remained. Seeing her, the young woman snapped out of her reverie. She quickly opened the door, smiling warmly. "Good morning! How are you today? Better than ever?"

The old lady paused, surprised. Her cautious gaze softened slightly. "Do we know each other?" she asked hesitantly.

Joy chuckled. "We didn't until now," she said, "but now we do." She introduced herself and invited the woman inside. They exchanged pleasantries as they stepped into the library together, and the elderly woman, still studying Joy's face for any ill intentions, slowly accepted her kindness. With a simple farewell, Joy wished her a good day and went in search of her own solace.

She found herself wandering toward the self-help section, hungry for wisdom. A book titled In Search of the Lost Self caught her attention. She barely had a chance to read a line when a familiar voice broke her concentration.

"Would you like a cup of tea?" the old lady asked, now standing beside her. The harshness had vanished from her face, replaced with a gentle warmth. "I've read that book," she added. "It's quite personal view of the author, but if you pay close attention, you'll realize you already know most of it. It's just that sometimes, hearing it from someone else makes you believe it."

She smiled knowingly.

"Interesting," Joy replied, her spirits lifted. "Please, have a seat. I'd love to hear your thoughts."

They found a quiet corner and sat together. The old lady began sharing stories of her life, her children, and the joys she had learned to find in solitude. Her voice carried wisdom as she spoke of how she had spent her youth caring for others, cooking for the less fortunate, and cherishing the close-knit community that once was. "The city has changed," she said with a hint of sadness, "and so have the people. There's less love, less connection. But today, your greeting brought me back to those days."

What a charming old lady. Her blue eyes shimmered with emotion as she offered one last piece of advice. "Remember, what you're looking for isn't in books. It's right here," she said, touching her heart. "Don't seek love outside yourself, or you'll always be disappointed."

Joy admired with a soft smile, her heart filling with hope. She had found something far more precious than she had been seeking.

Magic Pen

Children often don't understand the adults' world. What's even more interesting is that adults forget that they once were the very same children, amazed and confused by grown-ups' behavior.

It was a cold winter; my son was only 8. We were almost done with the New year's gift shopping. That day, my son bought a pen. Not just any pen—it was an invisible ink pen, or as he called it, his "Magic Pen." The pen's magic lay in its ability to write invisibly, only revealing the text under a special glow-in-the-dark light. He was extremely happy.

The first thing he did with his new treasure was to draw a picture on my hand. I found it delightful. His drawing was of one of his favorite puppet characters from a beloved book that he drew almost ten times a day, proudly talking about it to anyone who would listen. He was overjoyed, eager to show his magical pen to everyone he met.

Later in the afternoon, I took him to his music class. The class hadn't started yet, and he was bursting with excitement. He ran up to one of his classmate's fathers, who was waiting nearby, and enthusiastically said, "Would you like me to draw a magic picture on your hand?" Without waiting for a reply, he moved closer, ready to share his wonder.

The father, looking bewildered, instinctively stepped back and replied sharply, "No!" My son began to explain, hoping to clarify, but I saw the man's expression grow more defensive. Wanting to diffuse the situation, I firmly called my son back, saying, "Come here and sit down," adding in a more authoritative tone, "That wasn't polite; you shouldn't bother people."

My son looked at me in disbelief. "But Mom, it's really cool…" he began, but I interrupted, "Maybe you should give me your pen. I'll give it back when we get home." He sank into his chair, whispering, "No!" before growing silent.

I felt a pang of frustration. For a moment, I thought he had been impolite, and I was embarrassed by his behavior. At the same time, I felt hurt by the gentleman's reaction. Taking a deep breath, I sat quietly, trying to process everything.

After a few minutes, I glanced at my son. He was quietly drawing with his pen, lost in his own imaginative world, creating stories as he always did. His class began, and I sat alone in the waiting room, my thoughts swirling.

My mind drifted back to when I was eight. How much had I longed to share my excitement and joy with everyone around me? How often did adults react just like I had that day, unintentionally disappointing me? Even now, the memories can still sting. At what point in my life had I forgotten that the most beautiful moments are those fleeting, magical ones? When did I stop remembering that a simple pen could make the world feel so bright and full of wonder? Where had I lost sight of the idea that the happiness of a child is more valuable than anything else?

I felt a deep sense of shame. I had acted unfairly toward my little boy, whose pure joy and innocence deserved to be cherished. I should have been kinder ,and more patient .Perhaps even joined him in sharing his excitement and explained to the gentleman what the magic pen was all about.

As I sat there, memories of my own childhood came flooding back—vivid recollections of simple, heartwarming joys. Oh, how precious a new notebook was, a chocolate treat, or a birthday dress I'd worn until it no longer fit. I remembered reading Tintin and Snowy stories, going to the fair after six months, or a family trip to Mashhad or Isfahan. What a vast, wondrous world it was! That world had gradually faded, replaced by the clamor and responsibilities of adulthood.

And now, here was my son, experiencing his childhood. When his class ended, he bounded out with joy, proudly telling me how he had drawn a heart on his music teacher's hand. The teacher, smiling warmly, thanked him, and I couldn't help but smile back.

I held my son's small, warm hand as we walked down the stairs together. He clutched his magic pen tightly, his eyes sparkling with laughter. Forgiveness, it seemed, was effortless for him. The frustrations of earlier had vanished from his mind.

I have learnt so much from him! He brings me such joy and wonder. His gentle spirit and boundless curiosity have reawakened something within me, reminding me to reconnect with what truly matters—the essence of this life, the love that endures.

"Mom! Can we get some ice cream?" he asked, looking up at me with hopeful eyes. I looked at him and saw only pure love.

Through Another's Eyes

The café had been bustling for over two hours as I sat there, waiting. Conversations buzzed around me, cups clinked steadily, and though I had brought a book, I found myself doing what I often do—watching people. There's something about observing quiet moments in others' lives that makes me feel more connected to the world.

The line at the counter was long, and the young woman managing the orders moved slowly, deliberately. Her expression was blank, distant—almost as if she were somewhere else entirely. Frustration began to ripple through the crowd. Impatient customers exchanged glances, sighed heavily, or made sharp comments under their breath. But the young woman didn't react. She simply carried on, focused and steady, almost detached.

Then an elderly man approached the counter, leaning on a cane. He moved with care and smiled warmly at her. "How are you doing?" he asked, his voice kind and familiar. "When did you come back? We've missed you. I've been asking about your health these past three weeks…"

The air shifted. The irritation in the line seemed to quiet. The young woman looked up at him, and for the first time, something in her softened. She nodded, thanked him, and smiled—a real, weary smile. That's when I truly saw her.

Her face was delicate, framed by olive-colored hair pulled back into a simple ponytail. Her blue eyes—clear yet shadowed—held a tiredness that no sleep could fix. She wore no makeup, no mask to hide the weight she was carrying. Only the quiet presence of someone enduring something unseen, something private and exhausting.

And I felt a deep sense of shame.

We—the customers, the busy souls waiting for coffee and comfort—had been too quick to judge. We'd seen only her slowness, not her pain. We had assumed indifference or incompetence, never considering that she might be carrying a burden heavier than we could imagine. She didn't have a cane. She didn't stumble. She didn't weep. And so, we assumed she was fine.

But pain doesn't always show. Struggles often live in silence, hidden beneath calm faces and quiet movements.

We had made room for the elderly man with his walking stick, as we should have. We showed him the care and respect he deserved. But that moment made me realize: kindness should never be conditional on what we can see.

The young woman's resilience—her ability to show up, to keep going without complaint—was a kind of strength I had overlooked. She reminded me that empathy is needed everywhere, not just for those whose pain is visible, but for everyone. Because every person we meet is carrying something, and most of the time, we'll never know what it is.

YOLO

A message from Zara appeared on the phone screen:

-What do you mean?

I didn't understand what she was saying. I wrote back, -What do you mean what do I mean, dear?

She replied, 'The message you just sent!'

I hadn't sent any messages to Zara. I had a busy day and my son had been on my phone for the past couple hours. In surprise, I checked the messages and saw that a message had been sent from me to Zara and a few other friends. The message read:

"YOLO"

I turned to my son; "So?" With his innocent and simple laughter, he said, "I was bored and it just happened."

I wasn't happy with what he had done, "What does YOLO mean?" I asked.

"I don't really know. I heard it in a movie or read it somewhere." His cheerful voice turned into an innocent sob, and he sadly said, "I am sorry. It was only a friendly message, I did not know it was bad."

My heart trembled at his sad voice, but I had to firmly teach him that he had done something wrong. So, I continued, "My dear, especially since you don't know what it means, what you did is even worse. Now I have to apologize to everyone on behalf of both of us. Also, you broke my trust, and that wasn't right."

There was silence. His father, who had been busy with his phone for a few minutes and hadn't said anything, broke the silence:

'YOLO means You Only Live Once!'

I held my breath! It felt like a fire was ignited in my head, but my whole body was frozen! I repeated to myself, "You only live once!"

My son asked fearfully, "What does it mean? Is it something bad?" Suddenly, all my anger, frustration, and motherly disciplinary feelings collapsed. A mix of different emotions, along with shame, filled me. I said, "No, my dear, it's a very beautiful and true phrase. It means we should value every moment because we only live once and have no chance to make up for lost time."

He was happy and said: "So I did a good thing." I couldn't respond. It was like my lips were sewn shut. His father answered, "Your message wasn't bad, but what you did was wrong and shouldn't be repeated. From now on, find out the meaning of something before using it, and ask for permission before doing something of that sort."

My son wrapped his soft and chubby arms around my neck, kissed my face with all his love, and said again, "I am sorry, mom!" I hugged him: "It's okay. The important thing is that we all learnt our lesson and won't repeat it."

It felt like a heavy peace poured into my soul. We spent the next hour in silence and calm.

That night, I sobbed and cried quietly. I spent hours thinking about the walls I had built around myself. About something that was lost inside me! Like everyone else, I had fallen many times in my life and stood up again. I had countless unforgettable happy memories and countless passing sorrows. I focused so much on the beauty and love in life so that no pain or wound could bring me down. I looked up to the living heroes of my life and the ever-living heroes of history. Whenever I felt sad, I laughed more; whenever I felt tired and sorrowful, I danced more. I tried to live by this line from Hafez, like many people I respected and cherished:

"With a bleeding heart, bring a smiling lip like a cup, if you get wounded, don't roar like a harp."

I experienced the feeling of joy and freedom many times. Many times, the doors of mercy and blessing opened to me from all directions, and happiness embraced me.

My father used to tell me: "Acquire a temperament that can build a world, or an ambition that can transcend through it." Once I asked him, "Then why you are not talking to your best friend anymore?" He sighed and said, "May your heart never break, my dear!" In those days I promised myself that I will try my best to forget and forgive. I tried to accept everything and everyone, just as others opened their hearts to me. It was so beautiful to be quenched with love and affection. I tried not to take anyone's words or actions to heart and not to expect them to be the way I desire them to be. In the times of sorrow, I repeated to myself: "This too shall pass." And it really did! Even though it seemed to be working, sometimes my heart got shattered and I just felt that I need to scream.

My dear friend Zara, is one of the strongest women I have known in my life. She was thrilled to know about the meaning of the phrase YOLO!

"WOW!" She said: "I am so grateful that he sent me this message. I needed to hear that and reflect on myself and my life. I shall make it up to him!"

She was right. There comes a time that we all have to revise some of our beliefs and deeds. I have lived with my feelings and in my feelings, and I am happy. Although I had often heard that I should not reveal my true feelings everywhere and to everyone. When I lost my dearest father, I decided to tell my dear ones how much I love them before losing the chance, even though they might not appreciate it. I believed in people and valued them as much as I could comprehend, and I believed in myself.

On a rainy fall day, I realized a painful reality. I wasn't as strong as I thought. Eventually, I got tired of being wounded, of breaking. I had been broken many times, but the time came that I got heart broken and more than that; my belief broke, and I shattered from inside…

I built a barrier around my heart. I sat in solitude, in silence.

I asked God to give me a sign to rise again. And suddenly, my little angel, with a childish game, sent me a message of enlightenment. YOU ONLY LIVE ONCE! I only have one chance!

I reflected on the days gone by. On the words said and unsaid. On what I have done and what I must do. Something lit up inside my heart. I have been so fortunate. To see, to hear, to understand, to read, to write, to learn, and sometimes to teach, to apologize and to forgive. To be a companion and empathetic; And to love with all my being, and to want to be loved. Every day of life, every moment, is a reason for hope and joy. Our breaths are precious.

Sometimes, we put ourselves in a situation we do not belong to and struggle in vain to stay there. Instead of rising and freeing, we fall more and more, becoming trapped and drained. And no one can save us except ourselves... That dawn, I told myself, no matter how difficult, I can! I have to rise. The happy child within me who has always looked up to me with hope, or the suffering people around me who remind me from afar that I have an important reason to live and breathe.

...Today, I found her in the mirror. She looked at me with hope and love, and I promised her "I won't leave you alone!"

Opus of Life

The world of painting feels like a new, uncharted territory to me. The blend of colors is mesmerizing! Within each hue, I discover hidden shades, layers of stories waiting to be told. It amazes me that even the vibrant orange reveals gentle streaks of gray, softening its intensity. No color is ever truly pure. Pure colors, though striking, can sometimes overwhelm the eye. To make them pleasing, you must mix in just a touch of others. Balance is everything. With the right proportions, two colors can bloom into a thousand unique shades, each one captivating and distinct, just like people.

Ah, people! Each person carries within them countless shades and nuances. It's this mix, this blend of light and dark, that makes them beautiful. A soul untouched, pure and unblended, can sometimes seem too harsh, too stark.

Painting, like understanding people, demands patience. You cannot rush the blending of colors. Pouring too much into one spot can overwhelm the canvas, just as excessive intensity can overwhelm a relationship. Corrections must be made gently, layer by layer, allowing time for each to dry before shaping the next. If you add more before observing the layer beneath, the entire painting can lose its charm, and the damage might be irreparable, much like love, much like life.

In love, as in art, patience is key. You must allow the hues of your affection to settle, to breathe. Rushing can leave you exhausted, staring at a canvas stained with the very love you poured so recklessly into it. At that moment, you may blame the painting, the love, the people, but deep down, you'll know it was your impatience. Sometimes, less is more. A soft touch can carry more depth than a heavy hand.

Every canvas has its delicate lines, moments that require precision and care. These lines and dots, faint and scattered, might appear random to the casual observer, but a true art lover will see their purpose and beauty. Life mirrors this. The choices we make, the boundaries we draw, sometimes subtle, sometimes bold, are like brushstrokes. Some lines are meant for the world to see; others are drawn quietly, visible only to you. They hold you together, define your space, and protect your heart.

Creating these lines is a challenge. It takes focus, courage, and trust in your intuition. At times, the process may bring you to tears as you stand before your canvas, vulnerable and determined. But you must persist. If you don't take charge and draw those lines, someone else will. Before you know it, your masterpiece will no longer be yours.

So, breathe. Take a step back. Trust yourself to find the balance of color and space, of love and life. Know when to blend, when to pause, and when to let the masterpiece speak for itself.

The Golden Heart

Love knows no boundaries. I remember my late father once saying that you don't need to be a great person or perform grand acts. Sometimes, a simple gesture can change the world. He often exampled the pyramids, not in terms of greatness, but as the work of countless unnamed hands. "Each stone was placed by someone whose name history forgot," he'd say, "raised by a mother whose name no one ever knew."

Susiana is another hero in my life. Maybe her name won't appear in any history books or perhaps it will, but I will always carry her in mine.

I was supposed to make her a nightguard dental appliance. That morning, I ran into her in the elevator. As always, she looked calm and simple on the outside, but her face betrayed a hidden turmoil.

"How are you?" I asked.

"I'm fine, if you can call it that," she replied. "You know, you have to handle each day as it comes. No use holding on to tightly by the way, I can't keep my appointment today. I just lost my job. Things fall apart so fast... I've applied a few places, just have to wait."

I nodded gently. "I understand. Life is full of surprises pr. Just today, a friend called to tell me she was let go too, and she doesn't even have half the rent money she needs. But I'm sure things will work out for her soon."

"Yes, we just have to have faith." With that, Susiana quietly walked away.

It was a hectic day, students were overwhelmed and the clinic buzzed with stress. Amid the chaos, the receptionist came into the dental office and said Susiana was asking to see me. I had to make her wait about twenty minutes, and when I finally stepped out, she was holding a small She was at the front desk, holding a small red envelop. On it, she had written:

A little something from a friend, just to let you know you are not alone.

"It's not much, but all I had for now." She said genuinely.

My heart tightened. Tears welled in my eyes as I hugged her. All I could say was, "I admire your generous and compassionate soul."

I was overwhelmed by her selflessness. Here was someone who had just postponed her own care due to financial uncertainty—yet she gave, freely and selflessly, not to someone she knew, but to a stranger in need. She gave, not from abundance, but from empathy.

True generosity is not giving what is extra in your life, but offering everything you have with sincerity.

It reminded me of a story my father used to tell. A

village man had only one sheep—its milk fed his entire family. But when a tired guest arrived at his door, he cooked that sheep without hesitation. **"He gave everything," my father would say, "because he saw the soul in front of him, not just the need."**

Susiana, unknowingly, saved a life that day—not because of the money, but because of the love and hope she inspired. When I handed the envelope to my friend, she burst into tears and said, "Now I'm sure that God has never abandoned me and never will."

Two weeks later, my friend landed her dream job.

"What should I do for Susiana?" She asked me.

"Pay it forward." I replied.

And just like that, Susiana became the first link in a chain, a chain of love, of unseen kindness, reminding us all that no one is truly alone.

I still remember something she once told me on a hard day "When you survive something traumatic, don't hold on to it too tightly. Just shake it off, like a gazelle after escaping a lion. Then move on." We shared laughter and sorrow, knowing that we shall do our best while we have the chance.

On my last day at the clinic, my colleagues surprised me with a farewell party. They gifted me a beautiful necklace with a pendant shaped as a raven's feather.

I did not know the raven's story until then. In ancient cultures, the raven was once a bird of rainbow feathers and protector of all lives. One day, while flying among the clouds, it noticed a fire burning on the earth. Without hesitation, the raven flew down to save the world below. In doing so, its beautiful feathers were scorched, turning black forever. But it became a symbol of wisdom, transformation, sacrifice, and spiritual awakening.

Susiana gave me her own gifts. A soothing cream for my ongoing back pain, and a most precious heartfelt letter. A letter filled with warmth, and that quiet presence that always felt like a deep breath.

Every word in her letter saw me. It was as though she looked into a mirror and wrote to what she saw in both of us; the human soul.

I will miss the shared kindness, the knowing glances, and the unity of souls in different forms...

A Stem in Love

There is a tale.

In a silent valley, a small and beautiful flower lives, a flower that wakes with a smile and drifts to sleep with a gentle sigh. Its petals never wilt; they say its roots are so deeply intertwined with the earth that no one can pull it free. The valley's walls have embraced it for centuries, and no one has ever been able to pick it.

There is a spring rising from the heart of a white rock, forming an ever-flowing fountain with the clearest water, pure, like a baby's heart.

Exploring the valley no longer fascinates anyone. People stand on the cliffs above, taking pictures with zoom lenses, telling their friends they've ventured into the depths of the earth. They capture the flower at noon, when sunlight turns its petals into a medley of colors. At its stem, where the spring gently wakes the tired earth, a rainbow appears , arching like a bridge ,over the flower. The magnificence of the moment is breathtaking. People admire its beauty, they praise it, and then... they leave.

Among them, sometimes one dares to climb down the slippery valley walls. The closer they get to the bottom, the more eager they become. But it's not easy. As the sun begins to fade, they look up, afraid of getting lost, of being alone, and they climb back out.

The flower remains, along with its peace and the spring, witnessed every night by the moon.

The flower loves all of this.

Years ago, it was named the **Queen of Flowers**, back when the valley walls weren't so steep, when people had time to visit, to sit, to breathe, to smell the blossoms. Back then, the valley knew the bustle of life. Now, the flower understands: times have changed, people travel far, stories are told through edited images and filtered glances.

And still, the flower waits.

For years, it has waited for a bird to bring the message of spring…

A smile to carry the warmth of friendship…

A word, a prayer, a caress…

The footsteps of a traveler.

It has grown used to waiting.

It knows this is the story of life, to stay, to smile, to be.

And for the flower, this is the most beautiful gift:

a secret kept between flower and spring.

One dawn, a traveler made his way through the rocks, where the spring emerged, and opened a path into the heart of the valley. He sat beside the flower, gazed at it with a smile, and stayed until sunset, watching it drift into sleep.

He thought to pick it, to carry it with him, but then he paused.

What if it wilts? I can't leave it alone. But I can't stay... I must go.

So, he tried to uproot it.

With his hands, he dug into the earth. The soil was heavy and wet, his fingers weak, but he kept digging; deeper, and deeper, yet found no root.

His hands grew tired. He stopped.

And then, he saw it.

A stem buried deep in the earth, drawing itself from the spring, a stem that was its own root, connected to the very essence of existence. He set down his bag and sat in silence.

Sometimes, the grandeur of a single moment can change a person's life forever.

A grandeur that no words or images can fully describe.

Maybe the sparkle of a tear contains it all, the whole sky, stretching toward infinity.

In a single moment, a person can become love.

Their existence, their gaze, their touch, and they don't even realize it.

They don't know, and perhaps don't want to know, how or when the feeling began.

They simply become... nothing and everything at once.

The traveler's hands slid gently along the flower's soft, steady stem. He placed the earth back where it belonged, drank from the spring, and prayed to the sky and the moon. He kissed the earth, and under the cover of night, he left the valley.

Sometimes, I visit a local art studio.

On a wall, there's a painting of a flower — utterly magnificent.

It's a flower of electric blue, with streaks of red running like blood through its petals. Its stem is as clear as water, and beneath it, the crescent moon glows in a radiant pool.

They say a master painter once came to the city — a man whose hands held the magic of light.

They say something miraculous touched him. He painted with his fingers, cracked and dust-stained. No one knew his name, or where he went. But where his signature should be, there is only one sentence:

"A stem in love."

Everlasting Melody

I know a lady, so beautiful; exquisite! Her name is Tara. She has a delightful habit. No matter the weather, her room's window is always open. Every morning, she stands in front of the mirror, combing her long golden hair. She sings, letting her voice flow freely as she reads aloud from a book, reveling in the joy of the words. Her voice intoxicates the sky. I believe the sky weeps and smiles with her.

Her weeping, like a gentle shower, blankets the uncultivated field of her surroundings. And then, Tara smiles. Her smile is part of her being, as if nothing could disturb her peace.

The neighborhood children tell a story their parents once told them. They say that when Tara was born, a nightingale kissed her face and vanished in an instant.

I wish Tara stayed in this neighborhood forever, but she is a free spirit. She doesn't like staying in one place.

Every day, I take a long detour just to pass by her alley. Her melodies soothe every loving soul. On sunny days, the light from her window is so intense I can't see her, but I know she sees me, waiting with her smile. I feel the melody of her laughter in the air, as if the world dances with her.

I don't know what secret she holds in her heart, but I know she's lived through tears and laughter, leaving behind an ocean of memories.

It's a long alley with strange neighbors. I've never quite understood what the word "neighbor" means. I always thought that someone who breathes the same air, sees the same horizon, and shares a common pain is a companion. But Sahara is a different kind of neighbor. She doesn't like reading books. She says there's nothing worth knowing in them; they're a waste of time. "Why should I let my life be shaped by the unknown?" She asks.

But her daughter, Ava, is lively and spirited. Her heart desires freedom the freedom to wander, to experience. Sometimes she writes, her words trembling like a shaky heart.

Sahara condemns singing. She believes it's a sin. "A voice that disrupts the tranquility of the sky is a sin," she tells anyone who'll listen. "I tell you, someone should put a stop to this nonsense. We live in a serious world; we don't have time for emotions, ideas, songs, and new thoughts."

I pass by her, smiling. Bitter and dark, Sahara accuses me of sin. I ask her how she knows what sin is. What does sin really mean? She rolls her eyes, her dry gaze fixed on me, and says provocatively, "Sin? Well, that's obvious. Everyone knows. It's written in all the books. Even God Himself said it!"

"Which book exactly?" I ask. "The last time I heard the voice of God, I drowned in its melody so deeply that I still hear its tune. Besides, in this unknown and tainted world, what can I do?"

I leave Sahara, infuriated. I must visit a friend who has just had a baby. I pick some colorful flowers, and the florist wraps them with a calm precision. "Mums flowers are beautiful in every season," he says.

I move away from the noise. My friend loves flowers. Her little daughter, Hestia, is sleepy. How delicate and lovable she is. I hold her in my arms, kiss her tiny fingers, and pass her to her mother. She needs to rest. Maybe tomorrow she'll smile at me.

On the way back, I pass by Tara's house. The fog is thick, and the alley is dark and cold. Tara's window is closed. Sahara says nothing, but her half-smile is cold and biting. I see Ava through the misted glass. I am sure she's writing something new. She smiles at me, and I can hear her thoughts: "Hello, Breeze. Good to see you again. Come back tomorrow. Tara will sing a new song."

I smile back, knowing Ava will be waiting for me. Perhaps it will be a sunny day tomorrow, and I'll bring Hestia with me. I know Ava will be thrilled to share the melody with her.

Butterfly dancing
On a candle's final breath
Stars witness their vow

Stella

"Make a wish!" He said.

"Perhaps it's just a single moment, Like the descent of a bolide, Like the shining of a shooting star. But embracing that one moment holds the value of a lifetime of endurance…

Mom's voice echoed from the patio steps. "Stella! My dear, where are you? Come tidy up your stuffs while the sun is still out."

Stella had scattered her toys all over the middle of the courtyard. At twelve years old, she had to start making room for schoolbooks and give some of her toys to the younger kids. She was stepping into a new world, feeling a sense of pride. Now, as a young lady, she knew she needed to do her best, with all eyes on her.

Mom appeared with a few empty cardboard boxes. "Put anything you give away in these boxes" she said softly.

Stella got busy. She found a pretty silver-handled mirror, a gift from her friend Mary before she moved away. The sunlight glinted off the mirror as Stella looked into it, and in the light, her eyes seemed to change color. Mary used to say that when you smile in the mirror, God smiles at you, and when God smiles, a shooting star lights up the sky. Dad always added, "Every night, the sky fills with stars. You count them one by one. They wink at you and vanish. But one night, one star stays. It becomes yours. You live in its eyes, and it lives in yours. Then, you never count another star." Stella pondered these words, feeling the familiar ache of missing Mary and Dad.

A noise came from the other side of the courtyard wall. Curious, Stella raised her head. It sounded like new neighbors had moved in. A teenage boy peeked over, his short black hair like a velvet cap. His eyes sparkled with a special sweetness. "Hi! What's your name?" he asked with a smile.

Stella hesitated, surprised. It was the first time she had heard a young voice from next door. The previous neighbors had older children who had long since left home. The boy grinned. "You don't have to tell me. I heard your mom call your name—Stella! And wow, you've made quite the mess!"

He locked eyes with Stella, pausing for a moment before adding, "My name is Aster. I have to go now, but I'll be back soon. Wait for me." His father's voice called from inside, and Aster disappeared, leaving Stella standing still, lost in thought.

Mom's voice brought her back to reality. "Well, where are you?" Stella quickly began organizing. She arranged her books along the wall and busied herself with her toys, reminiscing over the little red carriage she used to push her dolls in, the fabrics her mother had given her to make dresses, and even a worn-out baby bottle. Her laughter filled the air.

She was in her own world when Aster's voice rang out again. "I'm back! Need help?" He leaned over the wall. "I tidied up my school stuff last week and gave most of them away. I haven't gotten this year's schoolbooks yet." He pointed to a stack of books nearby. "Wow, I've read some of these books!"

Stella raised her eyebrows. "All of them?"

Aster laughed. "No, not all! Just some." He paused, studying her face. "Primary school?"

Stella nodded, and Aster went on, "Well, the last two are tough—advanced for the next grades." Stella smiled. "My dad got them for me because I love to read." Aster grinned. "Well done! Then read for me too." They both laughed. Mom, watching from the window, called out a welcome. Aster greeted her politely, then offered to cover Stella's books for her. She bashfully agreed, feeling happy to have made a new friend.

The next afternoon, Aster rang the doorbell, holding a bowl of pudding. "My mom is a great cook!" he said. Stella couldn't help noticing the camera hanging around his neck. "A birthday gift," he explained. "I want to capture everything."

They sat by the pool under the willow tree, where lilac flowers danced in the breeze. "I think I'll call you Little Miss Blossom," Aster said, making them laugh. Together, they took photos, laughing easily in each other's company. Stella let Aster sift through her toys and books, eager for his opinion. For her, a friend meant everything, and Aster seemed to carry a whole world within himself.

They were busy all week.

They packed most of the toys into boxes and labeled them. Aster's handwriting was noble; he wrote on all the boxes, "A Gift from the Sky to Angels." They arranged the boxes by the wall to be taken by Stella's mother.

They kept some of the toys and interesting souvenirs. They laughed at the baby milk bottle. Amongst the clutter, there was a baby spoon, all torn on the edges with sharp teeth marks. Its corner was completely chewed. Stella couldn't bear to part with it. They decided to keep it together, saying, "This is ours, just for us, marked only for ourselves!"

Mom brought a green plastic box for Stella. They put the mirror and other trinkets, along with the camera, in the box. Aster wrote on it, "(Little Lady Blossom's belongings)." Stella said, "Take your camera. You'll need it." Aster replied, "It's safe with you. We'll take pictures together, and we'll put them in an album." With dates, places, and stories. Soon the album of memorable photos became a world of conversation!

Stella didn't know why, but she agreed with every word Aster said. Perhaps it was the simplicity and peace, the security of having a friend, a companion, a true companion. Aster was a mature teenager for his age. He had seen people from both sides of the coin; Stella had only seen the white side of papers, the bright side of people, and the beautiful words. They agreed.

Their world tangled together very soon—a beautiful world of those innocent ages, with its own special beauties, short-lived and fleeting tantrums, and the simple heartaches of school kids and teachers. They made memories, simple and sweet.

In her youthful world, Stella had many friends. She introduced Aster to all her friends: a kind hero, ambassador of hope, someone who was supposed to do great things one day—things others couldn't. For Aster, getting to know Stella's world wasn't hard. He just had to ask her to do something. Stella couldn't say one word: (No!) Especially to her dear friend! She only asked one word: "What's up?"

Stella always had a new story. Aster recounted memories; Stella wrote. The album of memorable photos and a world of conversation—there was no time left for loneliness anymore. Stella had written a short story that Aster loved. It was about a little boy who made a seven-colored water box from wildflowers for his sister and made hairpins from his own hair. His sister painted with her fingers and never used the brushes, because those velvet brushes were too dear to be used.

They used to make greeting cards together for all their friends and relatives on New Year.

In early summer, they would change the water in the small pool. In the evenings, they would set up a family picnic with lettuce and cucumbers. And of course, fresh bread and homemade yogurt.

As autumn approached, Aster would tell Stella, "What a pity!" Stella didn't understand what was so pitiful, but she didn't ask. Once Aster asked her, "Would you like it to be like this forever?" Stella replied, "Isn't it supposed to be? Why are you asking?" Aster took a deep breath and said, "No, buddy! Everything changes!" He was right, and Stella knew it. But she was sure some things would not change—if they were authentic...

Stella loved to tell everyone about Aster, and he, too, was warm-hearted, quickly connecting with everyone. He always said, "Lady Blossom, I'll be back soon." And he kept his word. Amidst all his stories and troubles, he always came back. Stella waited for him. Then, away from all people and friends, they would sit together in the simplest and most beautiful world, calm and serene.

During the day, they would reflect the sun in the mirror. In the evenings, they would look for the moon, and at night, they would count the stars. There was always a place where they could leave behind all the weariness of the world, not care about people's opinions, and laugh at their judgments. They could be children for a few minutes and just pour out their hearts. They were empathetic, understanding each other. Stella was a good listener, and Aster was a better speaker.

And that's how they found many audiences, beyond the small yard of their childhood days...

Towards the end of winter, when the snow melted, they laughed at the half-melted snowmen. Sometimes, Aster would say, "What a pity!" Stella wouldn't say anything; she was sure that next year, the snow would come again, and they would make snowmen again.

Until one day...one beautiful, sunny day. One beautiful and long day, Stella understood the meaning of "What a pity!"

Children's small world has its own affections and dependencies. What a pity! What a pity it's not eternal. One day, they hide their pure inner child behind the mirror! One day, they grow up and judge; one day they grow up and their thoughts and words turn bitter People get distant from each other; sometimes they're forced to, sometimes they stay but their hearts go away, sometimes they go together, not leaving each other, sometimes they stay true to their promises, sometimes they pursue shiny wishes!

Days of life passed quickly, bringing them to the world beyond the courtyard and the blue basin of childhood days.

Life entered its next chapter. It didn't take long for Stella's existence to become a permanent element, a reality that always had to be there, in any circumstance. Aster moved away from the neighborhood—just a few blocks away, but it felt like they were on opposite sides of the world.

Every night, after all his troubles, Aster would look at the sky and feel calm. Stella taught during the days, studied at night, and collected articles and photos, hoping to tell stories again. She waited for someone who was supposed to come. Someone who should just be there and listen!

'Please, give me only 2 hours of your time; I have something very important to tell you!' But Aster's world was crammed with different worries.

Stella just waited. She didn't speak, didn't complain, didn't take a step. The world around her was full of things she didn't understand and didn't accept. She did not want to change it. "I LOVE IT ALL…"

How quick the childhood dreams are forgotten!

The day Stella put away her photo album forever, nobody asked, "Why?" Nobody understood the intimacy of those photos. And most painful of all, nobody longed for those photos.

Memories are bizarre. Sometimes we laugh at the

days we cried, and sometimes we cry for the days we laughed. Eventually, a day comes when we realize that the opportunity is in that moment. We realize that some things are not forever, and we shouldn't pass them by. We realize that we can't go to a new garden every day and search for a different star every night. One day, we realize how lonely we are between a successful world and a world of loneliness, because what should be there, isn't.

That night, after a long time, Aster came back to Stella's home. He longed for their heart-to-heart talks, their little talks. In a world of a thousand colors, among colorful people, he finally broke down. Among continual successes, daily routines, and people he had gathered around him for his own sake, he was alone; Very alone!

In the small courtyard, under the willow tree, he stood in front of the renovated house. On the blue tiles next to the tiled pool, there was a small green box with a picture of a shooting star on it. Inside, an old camera, two dried lilac flowers, an old photo album, a storybook, and a little green spoon with chewed edges. He wiped the dusty mirror with the sleeve of his coat. In the mirror, he saw the image of a young man, with velvet hair slightly thinning on his temples. Above his head, a cloudy sky, without any stars.

And he just thought, "What a pity!"

Zohreh Ansari

"Never" fades away,
Life dances in shifting light,
Fate's path sways our way

Love's Secret Prayer

I cried out, "Don't bite the apple."
You kissed it passionately,
and I awoke on a lush, green soil.

The sky tenderly unfolds its blue embrace, setting the sun to flow through every moment. And so, I rise from every ray of light! From each shining window, I gather drops of hope, pulling life into my arms once more.

Oh, my Lord! This eager child and I, with a hundred ears and eyes, entrust ourselves to your enchanting story, guided by the light of love. Show me the way and unveil this secret, for it is laden with a thousand mysteries and yearns deeply in my heart!

If I must climb the rope to love, let me take its lead. And if I must soar, give me wings so I may rise above the sky. Should I remain hidden behind the curtain, then open my heart before I draw my last breath on this green grass.

Oh, my Lord! Isn't this life but a dream, leaving behind images of every fleeting vision? How beautifully each dawn and dusk draw a new horizon before my eyes! May the end of this dream fold in the embrace of the Beloved, where love's gentle whispers cradle my soul.

Oh, God! Help me let go; for the key to happiness lies

in surrendering oneself, losing oneself in love. Keep me free from suffering and safe from causing harm. Let me escape from pride and be established among the good.

Once I accept what I am and become what destiny intends, let me refrain from desires beyond my fate and providence. Find me, so I won't be intoxicated by success or shattered by failure.

Grant me the wisdom to remember that every moment is transient. Oh, God! I know my treasure is hidden in my heart, where the soul of the world flows in its clarity. Make me my own mirror and the bearer of my reflection!

Oh, God! Set me free from your bonds. While I remain a captive in this cage, I am anguished, and when I lack freedom, I ache. This cage was made for dying—set my soul free, like a bird soaring into infinity.

Oh, God! I have fell and risen many times. With each fall, my earth draws closer to your sky, and my hands reach higher. Behind every heartbreak, I have built a larger heart from the bonds of particles. Empower me to keep my courage and faith, and grant me the dignity to preserve my soul. May I never tether myself to the transient, knowing it holds no permanence.

Drown me in a sea with no end, for there is nothing but love, only love. When I find peace in this endless ocean, may I become the eternal spring of peace.

Soulmate

In quest, I searched with empty hands,
Unaware of the treasure that time expands
Now I see — your presence was the key,
To the lost part of my soul inside of me

My Compassionate One. My Kindred Spirit…

In the tranquility of your voice, I heard a soul; crying, echoing through the depths. You said, "Pray for me."

I held my breath in my heart, hid the lament, and wept with you…

But I hadn't told you:

I want to smile upon you like the sun each morning to offer warmth and healing, to wrap the sparks of my soul around you, so your tree may bear fruit.

I want to stretch your arms, crystalline in the rays of light toward the sky, to make you greener as you walk beneath the garden's shadow.

I want to become the breeze, swaying through your branches at dawn, to kiss your face, to dance with your dew, to carry the melody of your living voice to the open fields.

And when I return, I want to drown the sprouting saplings beside you in kisses.

I want to be the rain, to wash the dust from your face, to sit at your feet, to embrace your roots and flow with you into the stillness at the heart of the earth, to bind you to life so that drought and desert become only myths.

I want to be the moon, pouring light upon you each night, watching the peace of your being from afar, catching the reflection of your eyes in the vastness.

And when the tired waves gently play along the shore, I want to carry you and the boats resting on your heart to a safe haven.

Alone and calm, I want to gaze at you after the rain brimming with happiness, overflowing with love, with a single deep breath.

With me, and in me; like air in every breath…
I become one with your breathing. You flow through me.

You cannot lose me; I have found myself in you. There is no parting. We must let go of this feeling of loneliness trapped in the heart's cage.

Let's shed what we are and what we are not.
What we have and what we lack.
What should be and what should not.
Let us clear the mirrors.

Let us witness the radiance of life beyond this body,

beyond this form, beyond the dust of the sky, from the land of light.

Let us leave nothing behind but kindness and forgiveness for the heartened, for the lovers who embrace on the shores of the sea, for the wanderers who walk the deep forests carrying green hope.

Let us leave behind nothing but the priceless gift of love and gentleness on the dusty pages of history.

Let go. Let it pass!

How free I am. How liberated! I don't need a reason to love you. **This** is enough. I am so full of you that I cannot find myself. Perhaps... this is love. Maybe I must go, let go of myself, and walk alone. Maybe there is no way back.

Maybe getting lost in you was what I sought all along. I don't know. But something inside me says; **This is it...**

Last Chance

The weary autumn wind stirred the waves of her hair, casting her tresses upon the rocks. The sun filtered through the clouds, creating golden streaks that turned the surface of the water into diamonds, sparkling with the remnants of rain.

"How beautiful it is!" she exclaimed, taking in the breathtaking view.

"It's truly lovely," he replied. "I usually walk this path so quickly that I hardly notice the scenery." With a playful laugh, he added, "You walk quickly too!"

She smiled back at him, the warmth of their shared moment brightening the chill in the air.

"It's a mistake we all make. It seems something is always waiting for us. We rush and miss the colors of the flowers and the songs of the birds."

As their steps slowed, he leaned in closer. "Listen! Can you hear the woodpecker? With its tiny beak, it deafens the heavens with God's might."

"What sound? I didn't catch it," she replied, straining her ears.

"Listen closely! A woodpecker strikes a tree more than twenty times a second. Wherever there's a tree, you can definitely hear it and the sound of their beaks. You can hear their songs too."

She focused intently, sharpening her awareness. There it was—a sharp, loud sound that she had previously overlooked amid her own thoughts. It struck her then, a moment of realization: why couldn't she recall hearing woodpeckers in the garden of her father's house, which had so many trees?

"How interesting," she mused. "My knowledge is so limited. But it feels like there's a message that needs to be sent sooner."

"Perhaps it's a prophecy, heralding the rain," he replied, glancing up at the heavy clouds. "They look full and ready."

They both took a deep breath and continued walking, savoring the tranquility around them. He seemed to know so much, and the way he spoke was delightful. They talked about birds, nature, life, and the chaotic world of people, sharing thoughts on the endless, often forgotten beauties of existence. They touched upon hope, smiles, and this very moment, savoring a brief silence together.

In every life, there's someone with whom words flow effortlessly, someone who brings joy that feels more precious than any wealth. A special person, a friend who mirrors your heart, with warmth and passion that connects you to something beyond the mundane.

This is someone you can speak with about the colors of the horizon forever, never growing tired of the conversation. When they're present, everything else fades away; you want only to be with them, to share space and time, to hear their voice even if you say nothing in return. You know they understand you deeply, as if reading you like a book, even without a word spoken. They are the one you confide in, whether they are near or far.

An hour passed like a fleeting moment, and as always, a sense of calm enveloped her.

"One question!" she said suddenly, breaking the calm silence. "If you knew this was the last time we would see each other, what would you do?"

He paused, feeling the weight of her inquiry.

"I would hold you tightly in my arms and never let you go!" He confessed, his eyes shining with sincerity.

The bittersweet taste of goodbyes lingered in the air, an unspoken rejoinder of the beauty and delicacy of their connection.

Endless Love

At some point in our lives, something comes our way, demanding the courage to pursue. It's true; we always have a choice! And this time, I chose to let go—and that took a lot of courage.

I've thought about it many times. Maybe I didn't consciously choose my path, but looking back, I see that I never tried to change or stop anything. I let things progress, let events unfold. Why? As much as I tried to plan and control the course of events throughout my life, it rarely worked out. It sounds cliché, I know, but when people say, "It's not possible," they're often avoiding responsibility. One might oppose; I'm not trying to change any mindset.

A long time ago, I decided to live in the present moment. Believe me, **it was not easy.** But something miraculous happened: I found a way to rise above complexities. A fresh love for life bloomed in my heart, a love for people, and at the same time, a profound lightness.

Somewhere along this journey, I told myself, "Let go." And I did. I realized I didn't want much, just one thing—and that desire grew every day. Courageously, and maybe even romantically, I cherished being with my loved ones. At first, a bit selfishly, but gradually, I wanted them for their own sakes. I craved to be with them, to share everything with them, to experience life with them. Even when they weren't physically there, their presence lingered. I made a promise, one that took all my courage: to always be there, no matter how hard! I kept my word...

Over time, I realized I was no longer needed. The pain of feeling like I was "too much" was beyond words. Nobody explained why, and I couldn't understand it by myself. The truth was harsh: too much love can be suffocating. Unknowingly, I had built a cage with my love, fueled by an ego I never recognized.

So, I prayed: "Oh God, help me! I don't want to hurt the ones I love. Let them be happy, free to live as they wish. Let me hold them in my heart, where they truly belong."

That was when I saw I no longer needed them to be mine. I wanted happiness for them, even if it meant they wouldn't be with me. I wanted them to have everything life could offer, even if it meant setting them free. Love became a gift I could share with everyone, nourishing others' souls and feeling nourished in return. Their passion, their joy—these became my reasons for happiness.

Then, life gifted me true love. A divine reflection of my soul appeared through another existence. I found someone who could be me, who could read me without needing me to say a word. I found you.

In my quiet solitude, I realized that I want you for yourself, for who you will become. My greatest joy is witnessing you shine brighter each day.

I cherish our memories and treasure the moments we've shared. I will always be here for you. Tears may be mine to keep, but with all my love...

I let you go!

...

Gardenia's Heart

From between the newly sprouted willow branches, a ray of sunlight awakens the pond. The fresh morning breeze weaves through the willow leaves, making the light dance in the pond's reflection. A shadow rests beneath my feet.

"You're so quiet."

"There's so much to say. So much…"

"Don't feel lonely. These distances are only an illusion. We are all connected, like a ring, like roots from one source. We never truly separate unless we choose to break the bond. Even then, we remain bound because our hearts are still connected to the same core."

"That's true. No complaints—like you said, it's just a moment. Everyone has their share, and fighting it is pointless."

"We mustn't fight! We live for reconciliation."

"That's right."

A deep breath… and silence. By the pond, from the tangle of bamboo reeds, a beautiful duck approaches, followed by four ducklings. Behind them is another duck, proud and poised, as if ushering in the new day.

"Is it far to the ocean?"

"We have to walk for a few minutes. It's good; we'll warm up, too."

"Maybe you'll tell me another story along the way."

Underfoot, the earth is soft, breathing the scent of dust and memory. A dove lifts from the top of the old elm, wings catching the morning light. Crows call in the distance, their echoes fading into the hush. Ducks slip quietly into the reeds, leaving only ripples behind. Just ahead, gardenias bloom in secret splendor, glamorous and glowing beneath the gentle sun, they sway with grace in the arms of the breeze, whispering spring's quiet secrets into the air. Their fragrance clings to me; sweet, unspoken, eternal. With every petal, they open their hearts, and mine listens.

The shoreline lies half-asleep, cradled between sunlight and shadow. Far ahead, the horizon dissolves, the sky and sea no longer lovers apart, but one endless breath, one silken thread of stillness.

The waves hush their stories; there is no edge between

them. And in this hush, I feel another beautiful story beginning…

One that already knows my name.

I shall never die!
Life and I;
We are entwined.

In the heart of each particle in the air,
My love and smile will appear

Zohreh
Autumn 2024

Zohreh Ansari

The moment you believe in love's sweet lore,
  Remember me, my friend; forevermore.

www.ingramcontent.com/pod-product-compliance
Lightning Source LLC
Chambersburg PA
CBHW061119070526
44583CB00028B/3338